Flick Your Heart-Light On, Let Your Fears Be Gone!

Helping Children Connect to Their Heart to Soothe Their Mind

Tonia Cianciulli

Flick Your Heart-Light On, Let Your Fears Be Gone!

Written by:
Tonia Evans Cianciulli

Illustrated by:
Sophia Josephine Cianciulli

tellwell

Tellwell Talent
www.tellwell.ca

ISBN
978-0-2288-9376-9 (Hardcover)
978-0-2288-9375-2 (Paperback)

A book for young children.
To be read with parents or anyone they love, and trust.

Early Praise for . . .

'FLICK YOUR HEART-LIGHT ON, LET YOUR FEARS BE GONE!'

'What a beautiful gift of a book. I only wish I had this book when my own kids were teenagers and experiencing anxiety. We all need to continue to take the stigma out of mental health struggles. Compounded by the isolation and stress of the pandemic we now have an epidemic of anxiety among so many of our young people. Tonia Cianciulli has found a meaningful, powerful way to educate, empower and enlighten the hearts of our precious children. Bravo. A must read for parents and kids alike!'

- **Laura Robinson**, Inventor of BALDERDASH and Emmy-nominated TV producer

'Flick Your Heart-Light On, Let Your Fears Be Gone is a game changer for children and parents alike. Tonia's ability to share from both her own parenting and education allows her to give practical strategies children can use immediately in times such as this. This is because anxiety is higher than ever. Five stars all the way!!'

- **Christy Primmer**, Author & TV Host

'Tonia's book sheds light into the dark corners of a child's psyche and gives parents and children the loving dialogue to see their way through. A warm hug for the heart and soul.'

- **Tanya Chernova**, Author of UNDERMIND, International Speaker, Co-founder of Courageous Living.

'This beautiful book gives me hope. It does something few books do — it offers a healing remedy for our armoured hearts. This is utterly essential to the co-creation of the world we long for. Highly recommended!'

- **Jeff Brown**, Author of Love it Forward and HEARTICULATIONS

'When I was young, I was artistic, insecure and felt very different from my peers. I had the Broken-Hearted Monster inside me. Tonia's gentle, uplifting book would have been a great comfort back then. Her reminder that sharing our natural gifts can make others happy, and in turn ourselves, really spoke to me. Encouraging young people to talk to someone they trust when they are experiencing doubts and anxiety is so, so important. I realize that now. This book is a gift that hugs.'

- **Nina Keogh,** Artist & Award Winning Canadian Puppeteer - Today's Special

You Are All Heart

Do you know what an amazing person you are?

Did you know that you were created to be EXACTLY the person you came into this world as?

God took His time and extreme care while you were in your mother's belly. This was to make sure you would be born the very special and unique person you are today.

Before you even arrived, you were stamped with a seal of approval.

Where is that seal of approval located, you might ask?

Well, it's actually INSIDE you.

It's your HEART, and it's filled with LOVE.

You can imagine that your heart is also filled with light. That light is something that will guide you for the rest of your life.

Think about when you flick on a flashlight that guides you out of a dark room, or into a dark forest. You can use the light in your heart to help guide you every day of your life.

You are going to find out how your heart works, and just how magical it is!

Your Gifts & Talents

You were assigned your very own special gifts and talents that would set you apart from everyone else in this world. And this is true for every single person on this planet.

We get to experience joy from the gifts and talents we each have. We also get to experience joy from other people's gifts and talents.

If you don't know what I mean, think about it this way…

Let's say you sing a beautiful song for someone, and bring a smile to their face. Doesn't that make your heart happy? You shared something special about yourself in a way that only you can do.

Then let's say that person paints you a beautiful picture, and brings a smile to YOUR face. Wow!

What are some of the gifts and talents you have recognized in yourself so far?

When you share one of your gifts or talents with a friend, how does that make you feel inside?

Be Love

As you grow up, you'll discover what your life's special purpose is. But for now, and throughout the rest of your life, your Number One purpose is to BE LOVE. A pattern of love in your life began the moment you were born because you brought joy into the world the day you arrived.

But, HOW do we 'BE LOVE', you may ask? You will have some of your own ideas you can add to this list but, here are a few to get you started:

Speak to your family, friends, and teachers with love in your voice and heart.

Take time to do kind things for others. You never know when someone needs a hug or a kind word to brighten their day.

Share the gifts and talents you were given, with the people in your life.

Share some love from your heart by being generous with your smile.

If there's something difficult you've been through, help someone else who's struggling with it. You can help them get to the other side of their hard times.

Send some happy thoughts to someone who needs an extra boost of love, someone who is sick or is having a tough day.

What other ways can you BE or SHOW LOVE?

The Heart-Broken Monster

Do you sometimes feel like you're walking through your day and all of a sudden the thoughts in your mind don't feel like they belong to you?

Those thoughts can actually feel kind of scary or even mean.

It's almost like a school bully has popped into your mind. I sometimes like to refer to this as the Heart-Broken Monster. The reason I think of it this way is because many times, people who are hurt can hurt other people. The sad part is that they might not even know they are doing it.

Do you know someone like this? Someone might hurt you with their words because deep down inside, they are hurting themselves. Sometimes we can even hurt ourselves with these hurtful words.

When this happens, it can steal the joy in your heart, right? Or it can make your joy feel like it's buried too deep inside you, making it hard to find again.

It can make you feel like you're being followed by a dark cloud and it's hard to be the love that you're on a mission to be. It can make you feel worried about sharing the gifts and talents you were meant to share with a happy heart.

Let's imagine the Heart-Broken Monster looks like this little guy. Look how sad he is with that cloud over his head.

Where Did The Sun Go?

Sometimes dark clouds cover the sun. We know the sun is still behind the clouds and if we sit and watch patiently, we will see the sun come out again. Sometimes, we feel sad and we don't know why. We feel like the bright light of our heart is covered by that dark cloud.

Some of your thoughts might sound like this:

I look silly today.
What if I say something wrong?
What if they make fun of me?
Why am I different?
What if I get into trouble?
That picture I drew is bad.
I forgot the words to my song and that makes me a bad singer.
No one wants to be my friend.
I'm upset with myself so I'll bite my tongue or speak meanly to myself.

Do any of those thoughts sound familiar to you? Do you have any other thoughts that have popped into your head before?

I'm having all these anxious thoughts
But are they true?

Where do these thoughts and yucky feelings come from? It could have been something so small that someone said to you, or it could have been a feeling of sadness you felt about yourself. If we keep that sadness to ourselves, and bury it deep down, it can start to hurt us. When we feel hurt or unhappy inside, sometimes we hurt others.

When we feel like this, there are lots of ways to keep our light shining inside, until the sun comes out again. You will learn many of these ways in this book.

When Your Heart Leaps

Did you know that EVERYONE has these kinds of sad or worried thoughts or feelings inside their minds from time to time? Yep! It's very common. There's nothing wrong with you. You're completely normal, and pretty cool too!

Even your parents experience this from time to time. Even the most famous singers or dancers or actors or doctors...anyone can feel like this.

At different times we might all have a Broken-Hearted Monster within us. When we feel worried or upset, we might hear the voice or thoughts of the Broken-Hearted Monster speaking up inside our minds.

Sometimes, this can make us feel what is called anxiety, or worry. When you have anxiety, your body might think something is wrong. However, it could just be the excitement of what's happening next or in the future. Or maybe you need to take some quiet time alone and slow down, or talk to someone you love.

Here are some things that you might feel in your body along with the thoughts that are racing around in your mind:

- A feeling like your head is spinning
- Maybe your hands are shaking
- Maybe your heart is racing or leaping
- A feeling of butterflies in your belly
- Or your voice sounds full of tears or jitter bugs

What are some things you may have felt in your own body? Can you use your own words to describe them, or can you draw a picture of them?

Don't Keep These Secrets!

I bet you want to know some secrets to make these uncomfortable feelings and thoughts disappear, right?

Of course you do! Because then you can help yourself whenever this happens and you can help other people too!

I have some fun and easy secrets to share with you. These are the kinds of secrets that ARE allowed to be shared with others! These are the kinds of secrets that can help you get your joy and your cool back.

Your gifts and talents will be shared and best of all, you will be able to return to feeling and being love.

Light gets rid of darkness, right?

Just like if you put a nightlight on in your bedroom so it's not so dark, we can shine a light on our scary thoughts. We can feel our joy and courage returning to us.

How do we do that? I've packed a lot of my favorite secrets into this book for you to try out!

Many of these secrets can help us get our heart-lights shining again if we are scared or sad. I like to think of it like a favorite line from a song I wrote. It's such a favorite line of mine that I decided to name the book after it. It reads like this:

'Flick your heart-light on, let your fears be gone'.

Your Heart-Light

Have you ever given your friend a high-five for something really cool? Have you given a hug to someone who needed it? Has someone given you a big hug when you needed it?

These are physical actions that send a flood of special feelings through our whole body and heart. These happy feelings can help us feel brave, and can comfort us if we feel worried.

Something else that can make you feel this happy is when you put your hands on your heart. Would you like to try that right now? How does that make you feel? Almost like giving yourself a gentle hug. Let's add one simple thing to that. While your hands are resting on your heart, take a slow and deep breath in and out.

We'll talk more about heart-breathing in a moment. But first, imagine yourself like the kids on the cover of this book. Imagine that you have a small light switch in your heart. Try taking your right hand and pointing your index finger to where the light switch would be in your heart. Now give a quick upwardflick! When you give a little flick you can add the rhyme, 'Flick your heart-light on, let your fears be gone!' You can do this anytime you like and as often as you like. Flicking your heart-light on can remind you of the special light within you.

You can flick your heart-light on when you feel nervous about talking to someone, if you are worried about asking for help, when singing a song or reading for friends, or asking someone if they'd like to be friends.

Heart To Heart Talking

Now that you know some easy things that help you feel brave, let's talk about sharing our hearts and feelings with others.

When we talk about our upsetting feelings that race through our minds, out loud, to someone we trust and love, this is like shining a light on those thoughts. This is like making them disappear.

When we feel safe talking to someone we trust, it's like our heart is speaking to that person's heart sitting right across from us. Isn't that a cozy feeling? You can think of it as a gold or rainbow colored beam that travels from your heart to someone else's heart. It connects you, and you can feel safe and listened to.

If you think of these worried feelings like baby monsters, they will disappear because they don't want anyone to know that they're hiding out in our minds. They scurry away as soon as they see the light coming. Kind of like when your mom sprays bug spray on some mosquitoes!

When we talk about our worries out loud, they lose their power over us. The monster's voices get quieter and quieter. They start to shrink in size and so do our fears. The sooner we do this, the faster they disappear.

Let's check in on our Broken Heart Monsters again. Have you ever noticed that when you talk to someone who is mad or upset with love, they turn that frown upside-down? Everyone needs and wants to feel love. Even if they are scared to admit it.

When we are having a tough day and our mom or dad or a friend gives us some love, it's like our own inner Broken-Hearted Monster gets a dose of love too.

What are some thoughts that have bothered you? Can you take a minute to talk about them safely, and out loud?

Who are the people you feel most comfortable talking to in your life?

Sometimes it also helps to talk to ourselves as if we're talking to our best friend. What would you say to a friend who was feeling some of these sad or scary feelings? You would speak gently, kindly, and lovingly to them, I know you would.

Just like we would talk to others with love, if they were feeling scared, we can talk to ourselves like that too. What kinds of things would you say to a best friend or younger sibling who was feeling like this? Can you try saying those encouraging things to yourself as well?

Spreading Love

When we take the time to do something kind for someone else, it helps us forget those troubled feelings and thoughts. When we see how much joy we bring to someone else's life, it's as if the joy that beams in our heart bursts the clouds away!

What's something kind or loving you did or said to someone lately that made your heart feel so happy inside? How did the other person feel? Could you see how big their joy was?

Looking For Love

For many years now, I have had a habit of looking for heart rocks and shapes everywhere I turn!

Have you ever noticed that when you look for something, you usually end up finding it?

Many years ago I was walking along a beautiful pebble beach, on the island of Newfoundland, with my mom. We were having a loving conversation. I looked down and my eyes landed on a perfect heart-shaped rock nestled among hundreds of differently shaped and colored stones and pebbles. I couldn't believe that I had found a rock in the exact shape of a heart!

Since then, everywhere I go, I have made it a habit to look for love. If I am looking for love, I am sure to find it. When I find heart rocks or heart shapes in funny places, I get a happy smile on my face. It helps me feel connected to my heart. It makes me believe that I am on a path of love. It makes me feel like my heart is lighting the way.

Now when I am out with my family we all look for, and find, heart shapes. It brings joy to our hearts and happiness to our day! Is this a game you would like to play with your family and friends?

A Thankful Heart

Did you know that when you have a thankful heart, you will find even more things to be thankful for? Think of making a snowball that grows larger and larger when you roll it through the snow. As you roll the snowball through the snow, and push it faster and faster, it becomes bigger and bigger. Maybe you have heard someone use the phrase the "snowball effect". This means that things that start out small can quickly grow in size, picking up speed, and having a large effect. Having a thankful heart works the same way.

If you sat down to write a list, or draw a picture, of all the things you are thankful for in your life, I bet you would have a very long list. I'll bet you could fill an entire Bristol board with things you are thankful for! At first, it might be a challenge to think of all the things you are thankful for. But when you think of them more and more, they start popping into your mind quicker.

Here are some things to be thankful for:

- The sun
- A cozy bed
- A family pet
- Your mom, dad, or guardian
- Friends
- Your gifts and talents
- The air we breathe
- Our hearts

- Our arms and legs that help us every day
- Beautiful flowers
- Sisters or brothers
- The ability to help others
- The food we eat
- Water, trees, oceans, and your favorite animals

At any time of the day or night, you can say a prayer of thankfulness, and be thankful for all the awesome things in your life. What other things are you thankful for in your life?

Does thinking of them make you feel good in your heart and in your mind? I bet you will start thinking of them more and more each day.

Your Heart's Secret Power

Did you know that your heart sends thousands of messages to your brain every single day?

This means that if you give your heart a HAPPY FEELING, that feeling travels to your brain and tells your whole body to feel happy and safe.

When this happens, your body is giving itself a kind of happy medicine that only your body can make. Someday in science class, you'll discover this happy medicine is called DHEA!

So, imagine that when your heart sends a joyful feeling to your brain, your brain then sends the rest of your body some special messages. This is so they can work together as a team.

These special messages are like safety signals. We could even call them love signals!

These special love signals travel through your body to tell your lungs that it's okay to slow down your breathing. This is because it's safe for the butterflies in your stomach to rest on a branch. It's safe for your smile to come back to your face, and it's okay for you to speak again.

When these love signals travel through our bodies, we can feel calm and happy. When we feel calm and happy, it is easier for us to follow our hearts. And when we follow our hearts, it is easier for us to share our gifts, our talents, and the love in our hearts.

So, HOW do we give our hearts a happy feeling? Let’s read on!

How To Give Your Heart A Happy Feeling

This is all happening inside your heart, so if you're worried about what anyone else is thinking, don't worry, they won't even know. This secret is between you and your heart. You are in the privacy of your own heart.

1 Put your hand on your heart. Imagine you're breathing in and out through your heart. Your breath comes into your body through your heart-space. When you allow your breath to flow out, it's coming out through your heart-space too! In through your heart, out through your heart.

2 While you're breathing in and out through your heart-space, play a simple counting game to slow your breathing down a bit. Count to four or five as you take a breath in and then count to four or five as you breathe out. Don't forget that your heart is in charge of your breathing right now.

In through your heart, 1, 2, 3, 4…Out through your heart, 1, 2, 3, 4…

3 While your heart-space is in control of the breathing part, your mind only has one job to do. Your mind gets to show you a very clear picture, or movie, in your mind. This picture is a moment or a time that you remember being soooo full of JOY or very cozy in your heart! Would you like to take a moment and share this special memory before we get started?

As you feel your happy moment, imagine that you are watching yourself in a movie on a huge screen. Picture all the beautiful colors, sights, sounds, and smells. Do you have someone you love with you? Maybe a parent, a sibling or a pet? How full of joy does your heart feel? How BIG does that happiness feel?

4 Keep breathing in and out through your heart-space while you hold this happy movie in your mind. If you get distracted, start playing your happy movie over again from the beginning.

Are you feeling the joy and happiness that this special memory makes you feel as you remember it?

The last step is to imagine beaming all that joy and love that you feel through your entire body. Beam all that love and joy so that it

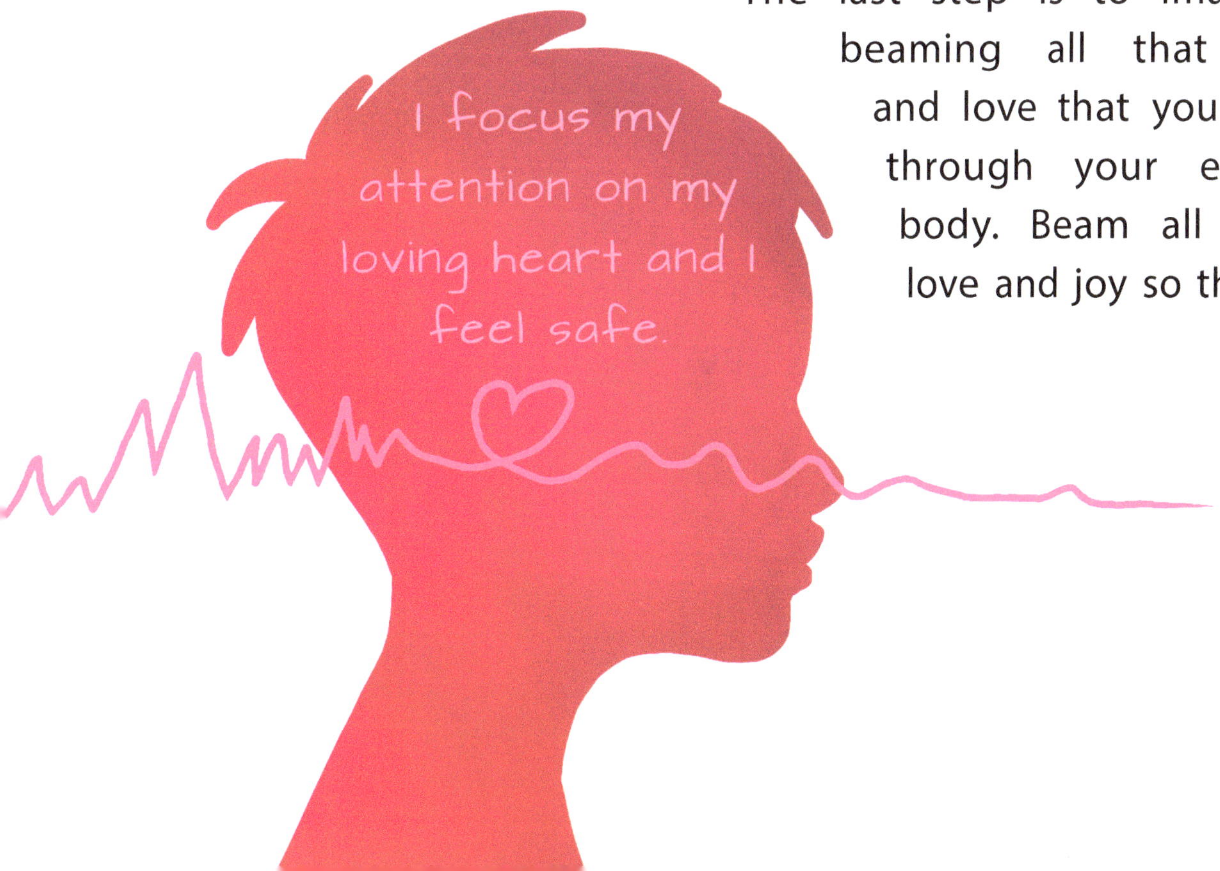

travels all throughout your arms, your fingers, your legs, your toes, your belly, your heart, your brain, your eyes, your nose and even your beautiful smile!

And now that you're smiling big, beam all that love and joy out across the room or the park or across your neighborhood. This is for all the people you love, and those who love YOU!!

What color was your love beam? Gold, Silver, Rainbow colored?

How did breathing through your heart-space make you feel? Did you like remembering your happy moments?

When do you think you could have done this lately? Was there a time in this past week, or recently that you would have used this if you knew about it?

What other happy moments can you think of right now so that you can use them another time? You can start collecting these happy memories in a picture book or in your mind.

Practicing Your New Secrets

You might need to practice some of these secrets until you get used to them. The more you practice them, the easier they will feel. If you have trouble remembering, just think: Follow your heart!

Remember too, you can share these secrets with your family and friends for when they need a bit of help or a burst of joy.

You get to share your gifts and talents AND the secret power of your beautiful heart!

You are special. You are loved! The world needs YOUR special heart, and the special way that you show love.

Author
Tonia Evans Cianciulli

Tonia is a mom of two awesome teenagers, Sophia and Anthony. Her children were in grades 1 and 3 when she began homeschooling them. Tonia is a Canadian opera singer and songwriter. She is the co-author of the award-winning book, *The Heart's Obsession – An Intimate Biography of Newfoundland Songstress Georgina Stirling*. Tonia has been praised by CBC for promoting her Newfoundland musical roots.

Her forthcoming album, Love Me Till I'm Me Again features the title track, *Thousand Cries.* This track features her and her daughter, Sophia, in the music video. Tonia is a certified Neuro Linguistic Programming practitioner, and a certified teacher with the Institute of HeartMath. She is also completing her master's in counselling psychology at Yorkville University.

The upbeat song featuring the lyrics, *'Flick your heart-light on, let your fears be gone'*, are from Tonia's song, *Red Carpet.* Also available on YouTube, and all digital platforms are the songs she wrote and recorded with her children, *Hold His Heart*, and *Always Her Home.*

www.WishArts.ca

Illustrator
Sophia Josephine Cianciulli

Sophia is currently sixteen years old, and is a self-taught artist. She enjoys working in all mediums of art, from painting to drawing, and writing. She's worked on the illustrations of several books as well as an animated music video. Collaborating with her mom on this special project has been meaningful work.

Kids Help Line:

Text CONNECT to 686868 from anywhere in Canada,
any time, about anything.

Or Call: 1-800-668-6868

ed